Williamson  Publishing

Where kids READ for the REAL world™

Bake the Best-Ever

COOKIES!

Sarah A. Williams

Illustrations by

Tom Ernst

Quick Starts for Kids!™

WILLIAMSON PUBLISHING • CHARLOTTE, VERMONT

2/07

Library of Congress Cataloging-in-Publication Data

Williamson, Sarah, 1974-
    Bake the best-ever cookies! / Sarah A. Williamson.
        p. cm. – (A Williamson quick starts for kids! book)
    Includes index.
    ISBN 1-885593-56-2 (pbk.)
    1. Cookies–Juvenile literature. [1. Cookies. 2. Baking.] I. Title. II. Series.

TX772 .W52 2001
641.8'654–dc21

2001025839

Quick Starts for Kids!™ series editor: **Susan Williamson**

Interior design: **Monkey Barrel Design**

Interior illustrations: **Tom Ernst**

Cover design: **Marie Ferrante-Doyle**

Cover illustrations: **Michael Kline**

Back cover photography: **David A. Seaver**

Printing: **Capital City Press**

Williamson Publishing Co.
P.O. Box 185
Charlotte, VT 05445
(800) 234-8791

Manufactured in the United States of America

10 9 8 7 6 5 4 3 2

Other Williamson Publishing Books by Sarah Williamson:

KIDS COOK!
Fabulous Food for the Whole Family
by Sarah Williamson and Zachary Williamson

FUN WITH MY 5 SENSES:
Activities to Build Learning Readiness

Dedication

In memory of my grandma, Golde Hoffman Soloway, who always had time to bake cookies and talk with me.

Acknowledgments

I'd like to thank my parents, Jack and Susan Williamson, and my bro, Zachary Williamson, who have been my cheerleaders through this and many other projects I have undertaken. I'd also like to thank my friends and their families who encouraged me and contributed recipes to this book, especially Melissa Burback, Lynn Separk, Jodie Sands, Megan Thomas, Kevin MacMurray, and Steve Haddad.

Contents

Cookies — You Gotta Love Them!

Have you ever met anyone who doesn't like cookies? That would be a rare person indeed! People of all ages perk up when you mention freshly baked cookies. And if people are in the house when you are baking, well, just notice how quickly everyone seems to appear in the kitchen. Suddenly you are the most popular person around!

Some of my favorite childhood memories are of my brother Zach and me helping our Grandma Golde (an awesome cookie baker) make cookies. As much fun as it was to help her with the baking, it was even more fun to sit around the kitchen table devouring our freshly made thumbprint cookies along with tall glasses of milk. We'd talk and laugh, munch and talk, and munch and munch some more!

You may be thinking this all sounds great, but cookies are too hard to bake: difficult directions, a floury mess in the kitchen, not to mention the amount of time it takes. Fear not. This book is designed for people just like you who need a little help getting started. There are plenty of tips and hints to help you through every step from purchasing the least expensive ingredients, to measuring and mixing, and baking and cooling (I'll assume you won't need any help with the eating part!).

Now, as a smart kid of the twenty-first century, you may be asking yourself why on earth you would bother to actually make cookies from scratch when you can buy refrigerated cookie dough ready to bake from the grocer. The answer comes in two words: taste and YOU!

Admittedly those premade cookie doughs taste better than most packaged cookies, but they are nothing like from-scratch homemade cookies. And, well, what about you? Need I say more? You — and your own way of doing things — are the most important ingredients, by far!

After making a batch of homemade cookies, you will notice how good the kitchen smells (hmmm), how utterly delicious your cookies taste (yumm), and what a sense of accomplishment you get from a job well done (pat on the back). These are all things you won't find at a grocery store, even if you could buy a cookie as good as homemade — which you can't!

So, dig in to some of the greatest cookie recipes around. Baked and perfected by my family and my friends' families, these best-ever cookies will knock your socks off!

Eleven Frequently Asked Questions about Baking Cookies ... with Sarah's Answers!

1. **I'm 10 years old but I'm not allowed to use the stove or oven yet. Do you think that's fair?**

The number one rule for kids cooking is to *"follow the house rules."* If that means not using the oven without an adult present, then that is the way it will be.

The good news is that you can still bake cookies. Show the recipe to an adult and ask if you can use the ingredients and the equipment mentioned. (If you can't use the electric mixer, you can beat the dough with a wooden spoon; if you can't use the stove top, ask for adult help.) Once permission is granted, ask for help if you need it, and follow the rules you agreed to. Of course, clean up the kitchen, leaving it even better than you found it! My guess is that once you show how responsible you are, you'll be allowed to do more and more on your own!

2. **This is probably a silly question, but does it cost a lot to bake cookies?**

That's a great question! Cookie ingredients can be very expensive, especially recipes that have a lot of add-ins to the dough like raisins, craisins, chocolate chips, and special candies. If you bake a lot perhaps an adult will bring you to a co-op or a grocery store that sells some of these things in bulk (you buy as much as you want from a big barrel). That is less expensive. And buy the store brand or the no brand ingredients; they are usually cheaper than the popular brands, and they will work just as well. Plus, you don't have to add all the extras into each cookie (see page 22–23 for how this works with one of my favorites — but expensive — the *Craz-Ins* cookies).

3. **My cookies always burn. Am I doing something wrong?**

Everyone burns cookies sometimes. But if it happens often, check these three possible causes for burned cookies:

✱ *Is the oven too hot?* To check your oven temperature, you need to buy an inexpensive oven thermometer (your household may already have one) and check it against the oven's set temperature.

✱ *Are you leaving the cookies in too long?* Use a timer with a bell when baking cookies, because a few extra minutes can result in burned cookies.

✱ *Are you baking on the lower rack or with more than one cookie sheet in the oven?* When baking cookies, you should bake only one sheet of cookies at a time. Always place the cookie sheet on the middle rack for best results.

4. **When a recipe says use the whites of the eggs, how do you separate them from the yolks?**

You can use this technique in all of your cooking, not just baking. Be sure to do this over a separate bowl, not over the bowl with other ingredients in it. After all, you don't want to try fishing the yolk (or the shells) out of the dough!

Over a separate bowl, crack the eggshell sharply against the side of the bowl. Break the egg apart letting the whole egg yolk slide into one-half shell. Some of the white will fall into the bowl. Now slide the yolk back into the other half, again letting the white fall into the bowl. Do this until all of the white has fallen into the bowl. Set the yolk aside to scramble later for scrambled eggs. Use the white as directed.

5. **Why do recipes say, "Preheat oven"?**

It takes an oven about ten minutes to get the temperature up to the specified number of degrees for your recipe. If you put your cookies in the oven before it is preheated and set the timer, the cookies won't be done when the buzzer goes off. Also, if your oven heats up slowly, the dough will melt rather than bake as the oven is gradually heating up. Not a pretty sight for a cookie baker!

6. **If I'm missing some ingredients, should I just substitute something similar?**

Actually, substituting ingredients when baking cookies is not a good idea. In a cookie, ingredients work together. Some ingredients are used to bind the other ingredients together and others contribute flavors. The real problem comes when you begin substituting ingredients in the dough. So, although there are lots of cooking opportunities where creativity is an asset, you should follow cookie recipes carefully.

Now that I said that, I'll give you this exception: It is usually OK to substitute some of the mix-ins, using whatever you have on hand (such as using raisins instead of chocolate chips) or some of your favorite flavors (such as grated orange rind instead of grated lemon rind). But for a great cookie, follow the recipe exactly! You might find a combination you never thought you'd like.

7. **I always get stuck cleaning up when I bake cookies with my sisters. Any ideas about what I can do?**

Here's a simple way to solve that problem: Decide who is going to be responsible for specific clean-up chores before you begin. To prevent anyone from backing out, write the jobs down. Then, do what you agreed to and leave the rest to your sisters. Next time switch chores so the same people don't get the easier chores all the time.

8. **My brother is allergic to nuts. Can I bake any of these recipes for him?**

All allergies can be very serious and allergies to nuts can be especially dangerous. Therefore, I would have an adult who is in charge of his special diet check each recipe to be certain you can make it for your brother. Sometimes, ingredients like chocolate, that seem like they wouldn't have nuts, actually are prepared in factories where nuts are present. Your family probably has some special ingredients they substitute for your brother, so perhaps an adult will help you make the necessary substitutions in these recipes. It sure is nice of you to think of your brother!

9. **I watch my weight, but I love cookies. How many can I eat before I gain weight?**

A healthy person should be able to enjoy some cookies for a snack, along with some milk and fruit. If you eat healthy foods and get plenty of regular exercise, you shouldn't have to "watch your weight." (Unless you have a medical condition, needing to diet usually means that you are overloading on junk foods, not getting enough exercise, or are trying to maintain a weight that is not healthy for your body type.) So, take care of your body — and yes, enjoy some yummy cookies, too!

10. **My dad is on a low-fat diet. He always eats the cookies I bake, so now I don't want to bake any more because I don't want him to get sick. What should I do?**

You sure are one super-thoughtful kid! There are ways to lower the fat in cookies, and — good news for your dad and you! — you'll find that most of the cookies still taste really, really good. Try substituting applesauce for some of the fat or oil or use one of the new low-fat baking substitutes in your recipes. It might take a little experimenting to get it just right. Generally, I substitute applesauce for half of the total amount of butter or oil. (For the baking substitutes, follow the directions on the container.) The applesauce tends to make the cookies more moist, so it works best in bar cookies that you bake in a baking pan, but you can use it for just about everything.

11. **Why do recipes usually say, "Cool cookies on a rack"? It's easier to just leave them on the cookie sheet.**

You're right: Moving the cookies can be sort of tricky. But while the cookies sit on the hot cookie sheet, they continue to bake, sometimes turning a moist cookie into a hard, dry cookie. Cooling cookies on an open rack allows air to begin circulating immediately around the cookie, cooling it more quickly and stopping the baking process. That way, you get a super-delicious cookie!

Cookie Baker's Basics

Baking cookies really is very easy. In fact, once you get started, you'll wonder why I even included this "basics" section in the book. "Bring on the recipes," you'll say. But I think that the best way to a quick start at anything you do is to find out a few of the ground rules. From there, it will be a breeze. So, here we go — all you need to know to bake, not just good, but really great cookies!

Grandma Golde's Golden Rules: Tried & True Techniques

Somehow, when my grandmother baked with me, it never felt as if she was teaching me because she just sort of wove these "rules" into her conversation. Since Grandma Golde was a GREAT cookie baker, I always think about her "rules" whenever I bake, so I thought I'd share them with you.

Everything in Sight: Assembling Ingredients

Before baking, put all of the necessary ingredients out on the counter. That way, you never get half way through the recipe and realize you are missing a key ingredient. Want to make the process even easier? Measure out the ingredients before you start, so it is just a matter of mix and bake.

Out of Sight Helps Get It Right! Putting Away Ingredients

Another of my Grandma's great ideas is to put the ingredients away as you use them. You'll never have to worry about leaving out an ingredient or adding one twice. Even better, you won't have so much clean up to do at the end.

Measuring Up

Carefully measuring ingredients can be tough. You might be tempted to say, "I'm a 'creative' baker, so I can add a pinch here and a dab there." Approaching measurement in this way can lead to disastrous results (after all, who wants rock-hard brownies?). With these few tips, measuring will be a snap!

✱*Don't measure over the bowl with the other ingredients.* Imagine what would happen when a teaspoon of vanilla extract suddenly becomes the entire bottle — yuck!

✱*Measuring wet ingredients?* Pour the liquid carefully and slowly. Although you don't want to measure over the bowl, be sure to measure close to it, so that you don't spill along the way. When using a clear measuring cup for liquids, place the measuring cup on a flat surface at eye level to get a true reading. Looking in from above can be misleading.

✱*Measuring dry ingredients?* Again, over the bowl is a definite no-no. Slowly pour or spoon the ingredient into your measuring cup or spoon. Then, using a dull knife, skim off any extra that is above the rim so that the ingredient is exactly level with the lip of the cup or spoon. Return the excess to its container.

Sarah's Quick Starts Tips!™

Which Shortening? Butter or Margarine?

There seem to be so many choices when it comes to a shortening-type ingredient; it's a wonder anyone knows what to use and which is healthier. I'll share with you what I've learned as far as baking goes: If you want the experience of the pros, use unsalted butter which they say gives cookies a more "golden" brown and doesn't have the salt to enhance some flavors and mask others. Margarine isn't supposed to be as good for baking, and it's no longer believed to be good for you, either — especially in sticks. Go figure!

Try using applesauce or a low-fat fruit substitute for part of the shortening in recipes (see page 8).

Bake the Best-Ever Cookies!

So Many Ingredients Can Be, Oh, So Overwhelming!

What a feeling. You sit down to a cookie-baking project, only to choose a recipe with what seems like *thousands* of ingredients. Fear not! Many of the ingredients are what bakers consider the "basics" because they are in so many recipes. These ingredients generally include:

All-purpose flour   Butter or margarine

Granulated sugar   Eggs

Brown sugar, light   Vanilla extract

Baking soda   Chocolate chips

Baking powder   Raisins

Of course, if just about every cookie you like has *peanut butter*, *coconut*, or *strawberry jam* in it, then for you that is a basic, too. The idea is to always have these items on hand so you'll never be disappointed when thoughts of freshly baked cookies are dancing in your head!

The good news is that many of these items can be bought in bulk or in store brands, and they store well.

Stir, Mix, Cream — What's the Difference, Anyway?

It all has to do with the dough. Is it just the dry ingredients that you are putting together (then you are probably stirring), or are you really giving the shortening and eggs a work-out (then you are probably creaming it)?

STIR: This is a gentle motion, usually used to combine together dry ingredients such as flour, baking powder, and salt, if they are not being sifted together. (To **SIFT**, you put dry ingredients through a sifter or a mesh strainer, which mixes them well and adds a lot of air. Nice and fluffy!)

MIX: Just like stir, only with a little more effort on your part.

BLEND: Usually you are mixing something soft like butter with something dry like flour. You want them to come together as one without any flour left along the sides of the bowl.

CREAM: OK, keep it under control, but now is the time to get those elbows really humming, because you want these ingredients to end up smooth and, well — creamy — but not soupy! An electric mixer works best here, if you are allowed to use one.

BEAT: Go for it! Now's the time to take out any aggressive feelings you may be harboring against the too hard butter or the lumpy brown sugar. And the help of a handheld electric mixer sure is nice right about now!

The Cookie Baker's Toolbox

Even if you have all of the necessary ingredients, you'll want to be sure to have a few basic kitchen supplies (you don't need anything fancy or expensive).

COOKIE SHEETS

Believe it of not, all cookie sheets are not created equal. You can bake on just about any kind of cookie sheet, but some make it easier to avoid burned bottoms. The basic rule is the shinier on the top where the cookies are, the darker on the other side, and the thicker overall, the more evenly the cookies will bake.

BAKING PANS

"So what about a baking pan for things like brownies?" you ask. My advice? Start with inexpensive pans (either metal, glass, or nonstick) in these two key sizes: 9" x 13" (22.5 x 32.5 cm) and 8" or 9" (20 or 22.5 cm) square. These will keep you baking bar cookies and brownies to your heart's delight!

BOWLS

You should have one large bowl and one smaller-sized bowl for combining ingredients. The bigger the bowl, the less chance that your ingredients will overflow. Believe me, I know from experience that cleaning flour and cookie dough off the floors and walls before your parents come home is no fun.

COOLING RACKS

You need one cooling rack to cool cookies, although two racks are nice.

SPATULAS

There are two kinds of spatulas: a plastic or rubber spatula used to scrape the batter from the sides of the bowl, and a bigger, flatter metal (or nonstick) spatula to move the cookies from the cookie sheet to the wire rack.

Sarah's Quick Starts Tips!™

A Little Secret!

Spray your metal spatula with nonstick spray before removing cookies from the baking sheet. It makes it much easier! No crumbled cookies for this chef!

MEASURING CUPS

There are two kinds of measuring cups, and honestly, you really do need both. *Measuring cups for dry ingredients* like flour and sugar are usually plastic or metal and come in sets of 1 cup, $\frac{1}{2}$ cup, $\frac{1}{3}$ cup, and $\frac{1}{4}$ cup or their metric equivalents. *Measuring cups for liquid ingredients* are glass or clear plastic so that you can see through the sides to measure accurately. You'll need a 1-cup (250 ml) measure.

MEASURING SPOONS

Measuring spoons also come in sets and are used to measure small amounts of ingredients such as vanilla extract, baking powder, or salt. They usually have tablespoon, teaspoon, $\frac{1}{2}$ teaspoon, and $\frac{1}{4}$ teaspoon sizes or their metric equivalents.

POT HOLDERS AND HOT PADS

Yes, these are absolutely necessary! At least two of each! Don't substitute by using a dish towel; you really need insulated pot holders and hot pads to protect your hands and your kitchen counters.

TIMER

In cookie baking, timing is everything. A minute or two too long in the oven can change your golden brown, chewy cookies into burnt, dry ones. I usually set the timer at about 4 minutes early to check on the cookies. And, if I go off to another part of the house, I take the timer with me. You'd be surprised how quickly ten minutes fly by!

ROLLING PIN

When you roll out the cookie dough to cut cookies into fun shapes, a rolling pin comes in handy, but no need to buy one. Just fill a large mayonnaise jar (or something similar) with water, screw the cap on tightly, and use that to roll out the dough.

COOKIE CUTTERS

Making special cookies shaped like animals, hearts, gingerbread people, and holiday ornaments is lots of fun. Metal cutters are best because they have a finer edge for cutting the dough than the plastic ones. No cookie cutters available? Get creative (see page 57).

WOODEN SPOONS

Wooden spoons aren't essential, although they really do make mixing heavy dough a lot easier. If you can, get a mid-sized and a small one.

HANDHELD ELECTRIC MIXER

This isn't too expensive if you look for a sale, and, although you can bake cookies without one, it really comes in handy. You may be able to find an inexpensive one at a garage sale or recycle shop. (Make sure it works and that the wiring isn't frayed.) Otherwise, just get ready to work those arm muscles (consider it good exercise before enjoying the "cookies" of your labor!).

Easy-to-Bake Cookies

Ready or not — and I know you are — here we go! Let's begin with some fun recipes that are great for new-to-baking cookie lovers. Some are baked in one pan, which simplifies things a lot (and takes less time, too). You'll be surprised at what you can bake the first time out!

The recipes in this section are also great for baking with younger kids when you are babysitting, but be sure to get permission from the adults before you bake in someone else's home, even if you are allowed to in your own home.

How Do You Grease a Pan — And Why Would You Want To?

Most baking recipes tell you to grease the pan before adding the unbaked dough. You can either use a paper towel with a little dab of butter or shortening (like Crisco) to rub over the pan, or you can use nonstick spray. When using butter, I grease the pan using the butter wrapper. Without the grease, most cookies would stick to the pan's surface. Of course, with many non-stick surfaces available, you may be able to avoid greasing the pan. And that would be very good!

Sarah's Quick Starts Tips!™

Cookies Holding Hands?

If you are finding that instead of a lot of cookies, you end up with one giant cookie, you may be placing your cookies too close together. It's sort of like when you are sitting next to your best friend in class — naturally, you are tempted to talk to each other. Cookies seem to have that same problem. To avoid "hand holding," make sure to place the cookies about 2" (5 cm) apart on the cookie sheet.

Secret Treat Thumbprints

(best first cookie-baking experience)

These cookies have been one of my favorites since I was a little girl making them in my grandmother's kitchen. Remember how to separate egg whites and yolks? Here you'll want to use the yolks and save the whites for another recipe (see page 7).

Prep time: 20 minutes

Pan: cookie sheets, lightly greased

Oven: 350°F (180°C)

Makes: about 36 cookies

Ingredients:

Pastry

2 cups (500 ml) all-purpose flour

2 sticks softened butter or margarine

$\frac{1}{2}$ cup (125 ml) granulated sugar

2 egg yolks

Filling

1 jar of your favorite jam or preserves

or 1 jar maraschino cherries

or 1 package chocolate candy kisses*

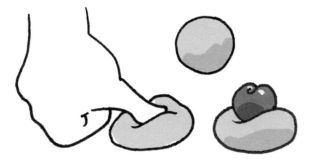

Putting it together:

1. Preheat the oven to 350°F (180°C).

2. Blend all of the pastry ingredients together.

3. Break off walnut-sized pieces of dough and roll them into balls.

4. Place the balls on the cookie sheets about 2" (5 cm) apart. Flatten each ball in the center using your thumb (that's the fun part!). Fill the centers of the cookies with the filling of your choice.

5. Bake for 25 minutes and cool on a wire rack.

SARAH SAYS: *If you are using a chocolate kiss for the center, it will melt in the oven (duh!). Press it lightly on top, as soon as the cookies come out of the oven — before they harden.

Design-Your-Own Granola Bars

These are so good you'll want to pack two in your backpack: one for lunch and another for an after-school snack before soccer practice or saxophone lessons. It certainly won't be your tummy grumbling as you score a goal or hit a high note!

Prep time: 15 minutes

Pan: baking pan, 8" square (20 cm),
    lined with aluminum foil

Oven: 325°F (160°C)

Makes: about 24 bars

Ingredients:

1 cup (250 ml) granola

1 cup (250 ml) quick-cooking rolled oats

1 cup (250 ml) walnuts, coarsely chopped

$\frac{1}{2}$ cup (125 ml) all-purpose flour

$\frac{1}{2}$ cup (125 ml) raisins or mixed dried
    fruit bits

1 beaten egg

$\frac{1}{3}$ cup (75 ml) honey

$\frac{1}{3}$ cup (75 ml) vegetable oil

$\frac{1}{4}$ cup (50 ml) packed light brown sugar

$\frac{1}{2}$ teaspoon (2 ml) ground cinnamon
    (optional)

Putting it together:

1. Preheat the oven to 325°F (160°C).

2. In a large mixing bowl, combine the granola, oats, nuts, flour, and raisins.

3. Blend in the egg, honey, oil, brown sugar, and cinnamon. Press the mixture evenly into the foil-lined baking pan.

4. Bake for 30 to 35 minutes, or until lightly browned around the edges. Cool the pan on a wire rack. Then, lift the foil to help remove it from the pan. Cut into bars.

SARAH SAYS: After you have made this recipe a few times, try designing your own granola bars by adding other dried fruits, nuts, and even candies to the basic recipe. Don't like walnuts? Try adding dried cherries or peanuts instead.

Butterscotch Brownies

These brownies don't rise high in the pan. Instead, they're thin and a bit chewy — just the way a butterscotch brownie should be!

Prep time: 10 minutes

Pan: baking pan, 8" or 9" square (20 or 22.5 cm), greased

Oven: 350°F (180°C)

Makes: about 16 brownies

Ingredients:

5 tablespoons (65 ml) butter or margarine

1 cup (250 ml) packed light brown sugar

1 teaspoon (5 ml) vanilla extract

1 egg

1 cup (250 ml) all-purpose flour

1 teaspoon (5 ml) baking powder

$\frac{1}{2}$ teaspoon (2 ml) salt

Putting it together:

1. Preheat the oven to 350°F (180°C). Melt the margarine in a heavy saucepan over low heat.

2. Remove the pan from the heat and stir in the brown sugar, vanilla, and egg with a wooden spoon, until the mixture looks smooth and glossy. Blend in the flour, baking powder, and salt until all of the ingredients are well combined.

3. Scrape the batter from the saucepan and spread it evenly in the baking pan. Bake for 25 minutes in an 8"-square (20 cm) pan; 20 minutes in a 9"-square (22.5 cm) pan. While warm, cut the brownies into 16 squares.

SARAH SAYS: Most households have either an 8"-square pan or a 9"-square pan. You can use them interchangeably as long as you check the cookies in the 9" pan sooner.

Light Lemon Squares

These are sooo good and sooo easy. And, they're kind of elegant, too. But they take a while to bake because first you bake the dough and then you bake it again with the topping. So, take your timer with you and remember to reset it to remind you to come back TWICE!

Prep time: 25 minutes, then bake 20 minutes;
Add topping and bake an additional 25 minutes

Pan: baking pan, 8" square (20 cm), greased

Oven: 350°F (180°C)

Makes: about 20 squares

Ingredients:

Pastry

1 cup (250 ml) all-purpose flour

1 stick softened butter or margarine

$\frac{1}{3}$ cup (75 ml) confectioners' sugar

Topping

2 eggs

1 cup (250 ml) granulated sugar

$1\frac{1}{2}$ tablespoons (20 ml) all-purpose flour

3 tablespoons (45 ml) lemon juice concentrate

Putting it together:

1. Preheat the oven to 350°F (180°C).

2. In a medium-sized bowl, blend all of the pastry ingredients together.

3. Press the mixture into the greased pan. Bake for 20 minutes.

4. In another bowl, beat all of the topping ingredients together with an electric mixer, until everything is well blended. Pour the topping over the pastry.

5. Return the pan to the oven, and bake for an additional 20 to 25 minutes.

6. Cool the pan on a wire rack before cutting into squares.

7. Sprinkle squares with confectioners' sugar.

SARAH SAYS: Put a toothpick into the center of a pan of brownies or cakelike bar cookies. If it comes out clean, the bars are ready. If it comes out with batter on it, you need to bake a minute or two longer.

Tea for Two

Want to do something very special for one of your grandparents or an older friend or neighbor? Invite that special person over for a pot of tea and cookies. Or, if she is house-bound and can't get to your house, ask an adult to help you pack up a tea-party-in-a-basket, and make someone very happy. (If you are feeling shy about this, ask a friend to go along with you.)

Here's what you need:

A small tablecloth or place mat	**3 tea bags**
A flower or some pretty leaves in a vase or glass	**Slices of lemon**
A teapot, if you have one (not necessary)	**Honey or sugar**
Two cups and saucers	**A little milk or cream**
Cloth or paper napkins	**Some special cookies you just baked**
2 teaspoons	**— like *Light Lemon Squares***

1. Set up your tea table wherever you are — it can be on a table, on the floor, wherever will work for your special guest.

2. Put some water on to boil (or ask an adult). Meanwhile, set out the cookies and napkins, the milk, lemon, and honey.

3. Place a tea bag in each cup or all the tea bags in the teapot. Pour the boiling water over the bags. Let the bags set in the water (steep) about two minutes, then remove.

4. Serve the tea, and let your guest add whatever she likes. Pass the cookies.

SARAH SAYS: If you don't know what to talk about, ask about what school was like when they were young or what games they used to play. They will gladly tell you. Listen carefully, and ask a few questions. You will both have a wonderful time.

Cinnamon-Almond Slices

Cinnamon and almond are two flavors that both kids and adults like. In this cookie, the flavors blend into a melt-in-your-mouth cookie. These are so easy to make, you'll be convinced that baking cookies is the hobby for you!

Prep time: 20 minutes

Pan: cookie sheets, greased

Oven: 350°F (180°C)

Makes: about 35 slices

Ingredients:

$2\frac{1}{2}$ cups (625 ml) all-purpose flour

1 cup (250 ml) granulated sugar

1 cup (250 ml) packed light brown sugar

3 eggs

2 teaspoons (10 ml) baking powder

$\frac{1}{2}$ teaspoon (2 ml) ground cinnamon

1 package (12 ounce/340 g) sliced almonds

$\frac{1}{3}$ cup (75 ml) vegetable oil

1 teaspoon (5 ml) almond extract

2 tablespoons (30 ml) cold water

1 beaten egg

Putting it together:

1. Preheat the oven to 350°F (180°C).

2. Combine all of the ingredients in a large bowl (except the one beaten egg), blending until the dough holds together.

3. Shape the dough into two logs, each about 8" (20 cm) long and 2" to 3" (5 to 7.5 cm) wide. Place the logs on the cookie sheet about 2" (5 cm) apart.

4. Brush the tops with a bit of beaten egg. Bake for 20 to 25 minutes until golden brown.

5. Cool on a wire rack and then slice diagonally into cookie slices.

Bake the Best-Ever Cookies!

Sarah's Totally Awesome Cookies!

You may be wondering, if this whole book is about "best-ever cookies," then what makes these particular recipes "totally awesome!" Many of these recipes are either new recipes that I developed (mostly by combining things I liked about other recipes) or they are recipes that were given to me because they were someone else's most-loved cookie recipe. To my taste buds and me, they just seem — well, totally, most awesomely, out of this world! So, that's why I singled these out in their own section for you to enjoy!

Craz-Ins

(oatmeal cookies with dried cranberries, peanuts, and chocolate chips)

In a crazy sort of mood? Then, *Craz-Ins* are the perfect cookie for you!
With plenty of chocolate, fruit, and nuts, they will please just about everyone.
My recommendation? Make these cookies with a friend. Turn on some fun music that
makes you feel like dancing or makes you feel a little crazy (my personal favorite
cooking music is old-school Madonna or Aretha Franklin), and get down
to the business of cookie baking!

Prep time: 25 minutes

Pan: cookie sheets, lightly greased

Oven: 350°F (180°C)

Makes: about 36 cookies

Ingredients:

2 sticks softened butter or margarine

1 cup (250 ml) granulated sugar

1 cup (250 ml) packed light brown sugar

1 teaspoon (5 ml) vanilla extract

2 lightly beaten eggs

1 teaspoon (5 ml) baking soda

1 teaspoon (5 ml) lukewarm water

2 cups (500 ml) all-purpose flour

1 teaspoon (5 ml) salt

1 package (6 ounces/170 g) English toffee (Heath bar or Skorr bar, coarsely chopped)

1 cup (250 ml) dried cranberries, chopped

1 package (12 ounces/340 g) white chocolate chips

1 cup (250 ml) peanuts, coarsely chopped

Yummy options:

1 package (12 ounces/340 g) chocolate chips

1 cup (250 ml) raisins or dried apricots (dried cranberry substitute), chopped

Bake the Best-Ever Cookies!

Putting it together:

1. Preheat the oven to 350°F (180°C).

2. Using an electric mixer, cream together the butter, granulated and brown sugars in a large bowl. Beat in the vanilla and eggs a little bit at a time.

3. Next, in a small bowl, combine the baking soda and water; then, add it to the dough. Lastly, mix in the flour and salt.

4. Now for the fun part — adding the goodies! Using a wooden spoon (to avoid crushing the mix-ins), blend in the toffee, white chocolate, cranberries, and peanuts (or any combination of these).

5. Put walnut-sized spoonfuls of dough onto the cookie sheet. Bake for 10 minutes or until brown. Cool on a wire rack.

SARAH SAYS: These cookies have a lot of expensive ingredients, but you can make them less expensively. Use toffee bits found in the baking section instead of those expensive candy bars. Substitute less expensive raisins for the dried cranberries. And you can buy most of these ingredients for less money, if you buy them in bulk. Or, bake these with some friends and ask everyone to pitch in on the cost.

Sarah's Quick Starts Tips!™

When Are They Done?

Drop cookies: Finding the exact amount of baking time needed often takes a little practice, until you get to know the cookie recipe and the oven you are using. Use your good judgement and when they look done to you, take them out. If they look only lightly browned, they will be chewy. If you prefer crispy cookies, leave them in a minute or two longer, until they are darker brown. (Here's a tip I learned the hard way: Cookies baked with dark ingredients such as brown sugar or molasses turn brown faster — and burn faster, too!)

Minty Miracles

If you could eat peppermint patties all day (like I could), then this is a cookie for you. And if you love Girl Scout cookie time mostly for their famous Thin Mint cookies, then this cookie just might bring tears of joy to your eyes! (And that's only a slight exaggeration.)

Prep time: 20 minutes to prepare the dough; refrigerate for at least 2 hours (or as long as overnight); final prep: 15 minutes

Pan: cookie sheets, greased

Oven: 375°F (190°C)

Makes: about 24 cookies

Ingredients:

1 stick softened butter or margarine

$\frac{1}{3}$ cup (75 ml) granulated sugar

$\frac{1}{4}$ cup (50 ml) packed light brown sugar

1 egg

$1\frac{1}{2}$ teaspoons (7 ml) water

$\frac{1}{2}$ teaspoon (2 ml) vanilla extract

$1\frac{1}{2}$ cups (375 ml) all-purpose flour

$\frac{1}{2}$ teaspoon (2 ml) baking soda

$\frac{1}{2}$ teaspoon (2 ml) salt

24 small-sized peppermint patties

24 pecan halves (optional)

Putting it together:

Initial prep

1. In a large bowl, cream the butter, gradually adding the granulated and brown sugars. Then, beat in the egg, water, and vanilla.

2. In a separate bowl, sift together the flour, baking soda, and salt. Blend it into the butter mixture.

3. Wrap the dough in waxed paper and refrigerate for at least 2 hours.

Final prep

1. Preheat the oven to 375°F (190°C).

2. Carefully wrap a peppermint pattie in a tablespoon (15 ml) of dough. Pinch the dough tightly closed. Top each cookie with a pecan.

3. Bake for 10 to 12 minutes, until lightly browned. Cool on a wire rack.

Bake the Best-Ever Cookies!

Dentist's Delights

(a chewy, chocolate-y, caramel-y bar cookie)

These cookies are delicious (even if you don't like nuts), but if you have braces, hold off on eating them, or you are sure to end up back in the orthodontist's chair!

Prep time: 15 minutes

Pan: baking pan, 9" x 13" (22.5 x 32.5 cm), greased

Oven: 350°F (180°C)

Makes: about 36 bars

Ingredients:

1 cup (250 ml) plus $\frac{1}{4}$ cup (50 ml) all-purpose flour

$\frac{3}{4}$ cup (175 ml) rolled oats

$\frac{1}{2}$ cup (125 ml) packed light brown sugar

$\frac{1}{2}$ teaspoon (2 ml) baking soda

1 stick melted butter or margarine

1 jar (12 ounce/340 ml) caramel topping

1 cup (250 ml) chocolate chips

1 cup (250 ml) pecans, coarsely chopped

Putting it together:

1. Preheat the oven to 350°F (180°C).

2. In a large bowl, beat together 1 cup (250 ml) of the flour (save the rest for step 4) with the oats, brown sugar, baking soda, and the melted butter.

3. Press this mixture into the bottom of the baking pan. Bake for about 10 minutes. (Set a timer so you don't forget!)

4. While the dough is baking, thoroughly mix the caramel and the remaining $\frac{1}{4}$ cup (50 ml) of flour in a medium-sized bowl. (Coat your spoon and a plastic spatula with a bit of margarine, because this can be sticky and a little difficult.)

5. Remove the pan from the oven — careful, the pan is hot! — and sprinkle a layer of chocolate chips on top of the dough. Then, add a layer of the chopped pecans. Lastly, drizzle the caramel mixture on top and bake 20 to 25 minutes, until brown.

6. Allow these cookies to cool in the pan on a wire rack, before cutting them.

Yumm!

How would you describe something so great that there isn't really a word for it — yet? One summer on vacation we were asking people in a small town which ice cream was the best, and one woman described the ice cream she was eating as "Very excellent!" Since then if something is out of this world (like your cookies will be), we say it is *very excellent!*

Sarah's Quick Starts Tips!™

Chips, Bits, Chunks — It's All Chocolate!

When it comes to chocolate, you can find it in all shapes, sizes, and prices! Technically speaking, what we all know, and love, and call chocolate chips are actually called *semisweet chocolate pieces.* Here's how it goes (usually!):

Chocolate chips, bits, morsels, and *pieces* are all about the same size. They come in lots of flavors: traditional semisweet, milk chocolate, white chocolate, toffee-flavored, butterscotch-flavored, and made from carob (a kind of chocolate substitute that doesn't taste like chocolate at all). There are also smaller *minichips* and larger *chocolate chunks* available.

Different prices may reflect the quality of the chocolate, but for most baking needs, the cheapest will do just fine.

Bake the Best-Ever Cookies!

Grandma's Best-in-the-Whole-Wide-World Brownies

You absolutely can't get these out of a box!
And they are easy to make, so I suggest baking a pan
before "Must-See TV."

Prep time: 30 minutes

Pan: baking pan, 9" x 13" (22.5 x 32.5 cm), greased

Oven: 350°F (180°C)

Makes: about 40 brownies

Ingredients:

1 cup (250 ml) solid vegetable shortening (like Crisco)

4 squares semisweet chocolate

4 slightly beaten eggs

2 cups (500 ml) granulated sugar

$1\frac{1}{2}$ cups (375 ml) all-purpose flour

1 teaspoon (5 ml) baking powder

$1\frac{1}{2}$ teaspoons (7 ml) salt

2 teaspoons (10 ml) vanilla extract

3 tablespoons (45 ml) light corn syrup

1 cup (250 ml) nuts, coarsely chopped (optional)

Putting it together:

1. Preheat the oven to 350°F (180°C).

2. Melt the shortening and the chocolate in a heavy saucepan over low heat.

3. Let it cool slightly. Using a spatula, pour the mixture into a large bowl.

4. Add the beaten eggs, and then gradually add the sugar. Mix well.

5. Sift together the flour, baking powder, and salt. Add this to the chocolate mixture and blend well. Next, mix in the vanilla, syrup, and nuts.

6. Pour into a baking pan and bake for 25 minutes.

7. Cool the pan on a wire rack. Cut into squares when cool.

Ooh-La-La's

(a scrumptious banana-chocolate bar cookie)

This cookie was named after a group of kids gave it the taste test. One person blurted out, "Ooh-la-la," after taking the first bite, causing us all to crack up in laughter. Since then we call these banana-chocolate bar cookies "Ooh-la-la's." You can almost convince yourself it's a healthy snack; after all, it has bananas in it, doesn't it?

Prep time: 20 minutes

Pan: baking pan, 9" x 13" (22.5 x 32.5 cm), greased

Oven: 350°F (180°C)

Makes: about 48 cookies

Ingredients:

$\frac{2}{3}$ cup (150 ml) softened butter or margarine

$\frac{2}{3}$ cup (150 ml) packed dark brown sugar

$\frac{2}{3}$ cup (150 ml) granulated sugar

1 egg

1 teaspoon (5 ml) vanilla extract

1 cup (250 ml) mashed ripe bananas (2 to 3 bananas)

2 cups (500 ml) all-purpose flour

2 teaspoons (10 ml) baking powder

$\frac{1}{2}$ teaspoon (2 ml) salt

1 package (6 ounces/170 g) chocolate chips

Putting it together:

1. Preheat the oven to 350°F (180°C).

2. In a large bowl, cream the butter, brown sugar, and granulated sugar together using an electric mixer.

3. Add the egg and vanilla. Beat well. Stir in the bananas.

4. In a separate bowl, sift together the flour, baking powder, and salt. Carefully add the sifted ingredients to the creamed mixture, blending as you go. Finally, add the chocolate chips and stir together.

5. Pat the dough into the baking pan and bake for 30 to 35 minutes. Cool on a wire rack before cutting into bars.

Bake the Best-Ever Cookies!

Lemon-Poppy Seed Way-Cool Treats

(This recipe makes beautiful, thin cookie-cutter cookies.)

Here's a luscious cookie that is habit-forming, so don't say I didn't warn you!

Prep time: 25 minutes

Pan: cookie sheets, greased

Oven: 375°F (190°C)

Makes: about 50 cookies

Ingredients:

1 stick softened butter or margarine

$\frac{1}{2}$ cup (125 ml) granulated sugar

1 beaten egg

$1\frac{1}{2}$ cups (375 ml) all-purpose flour

1 teaspoon (5 ml) baking powder

$\frac{1}{4}$ teaspoon (1 ml) salt

$\frac{1}{3}$ cup (75 ml) poppy seeds

1 teaspoon (5 ml) lemon juice

$\frac{1}{2}$ teaspoon (2 ml) grated lemon rind

Putting it together:

1. Preheat the oven to 375°F (190°C).

2. In a large bowl, cream the butter and sugar together, using an electric mixer.

3. Add the beaten egg and mix well. Set aside.

4. In a large bowl, sift together the flour, baking powder, and salt.

5. Gradually add the flour mixture to the butter mixture and blend well. Add the poppy seeds. Gently stir in the lemon juice and rind.

7. Using a rolling pin, roll out the cookie dough on a floured board or counter until it's about $\frac{1}{8}$" (2.5 mm) thick. (Chill dough if too soft to roll out.)

8. Cut with cookie cutters or the rim of a 2" (5 cm) glass.

9. Bake on the cookie sheets for 7 to 9 minutes. Cool on wire racks.

SARAH SAYS: See pages 56-60 for more ideas and recipes for cookie-cutter cookies.

Mandel Bread

(A sweet cookie, cut in thick slices, that is perfect for dipping in cocoa or tea.)

You've probably heard of biscotti — that great Italian biscuit that tastes so good when it is dipped in milk, cocoa, or tea. Well, *mandelbroit* (Mandel Bread) is the Jewish equivalent of biscotti. I think this recipe is the greatest because you can add all sorts of mix-ins.

Prep time: 35 minutes

Pan: cookie sheets, greased

Oven: 375°F (190°C)

Makes: about 60 cookies

Ingredients:

3 beaten eggs

1 cup (250 ml) granulated sugar

$\frac{1}{2}$ cup (125 ml) vegetable oil

1 teaspoon (5 ml) vanilla extract

3 cups (750 ml) all-purpose flour

$2\frac{1}{2}$ teaspoons (12 ml) baking powder

$\frac{1}{4}$ teaspoon (1 ml) salt

$\frac{1}{2}$ cup (125 ml) walnuts, raisins, or chocolate chips

Putting it together:

1. Preheat the oven to 375°F (190°C).

2. In a large bowl, mix together the eggs, sugar, oil, and vanilla.

3. In a separate large bowl, sift together the flour, baking powder, and salt.

4. Slowly add the flour mixture to the egg mixture, blending well.

5. Add the nuts, raisins, chocolate chips, or mix-ins of your choice. Mix well.

6. If your dough is sticky, spread a little oil on your hands. Separate the dough into three rounded loafs or mounds and place on the cookie sheet (just be careful not to touch anything else while your hands are oily).

7. Bake for 20 to 25 minutes until browned.

Bake the Best-Ever Cookies!

8. Remove the loaves from the oven, and cut them into slices about $\frac{1}{2}$" (1 cm) wide. Place the slices on the cookie sheet on the cut side, and bake for another 5 to 7 minutes, until lightly browned and crisp.

9. Cool the slices on a wire rack.

SARAH SAYS: This is a good place to experiment with flavors you like. You can mix in grated lemon or orange rind (lightly grate only the colored part without the bitter white part), dried apricots, dried cherries, dried pineapple, coconut pieces, chocolate chunks, or whatever you think might make an interesting cookie. The total mix-in should be about $\frac{1}{2}$ cup (125 ml).

Seafoam Chews

(kind of difficult, but too good to miss)

OK, so these cookies are a little more complicated than the other recipes in this book. You might want to wait until you are feeling like the Master Chef that you are before making these. My grandmother used to make *Seafoam Chews* and they were one of our all-time favorites.

Prep time: 40 minutes

Pan: baking pan, 9" x 13" (22.5 cm x 32.5 cm), greased

Oven: 325°F (160°C)

Makes: about 54 small squares

Ingredients:

Pastry

1 stick softened butter or margarine

$\frac{1}{2}$ cup (125 ml) granulated sugar

$\frac{1}{2}$ cup (125 ml) packed light brown sugar

2 egg yolks (save the egg whites; you'll need those, too)

1 teaspoon (5 ml) vanilla extract

2 cups (500 ml) all-purpose flour

2 teaspoons (10 ml) baking powder

1 teaspoon (5 ml) baking soda

$\frac{1}{2}$ teaspoon (2 ml) salt

3 tablespoons (45 ml) milk

1 package (6 ounces/170 g) chocolate chips

Topping

2 egg whites

1 cup (250 ml) packed light brown sugar

$\frac{3}{4}$ cup (175 ml) salted peanuts, coarsely chopped

Putting it together:

1. Preheat the oven to 325°F (160°C).

2. In a large bowl, cream together the butter, granulated sugar, and brown sugar, using an electric mixer. Beat in the egg yolks and the vanilla.

3. In a separate large bowl, sift the flour, baking powder, baking soda, and salt together. Gradually add the creamed mixture to the flour mixture, and blend together (gradually being the key word here).

4. This mixture will get thick and hard to stir, so add the milk and beat the dough well, into a fluffy light dough. Press the dough evenly into your pan. Lastly, sprinkle on a layer of chocolate chips and press them down lightly into the dough.

5. Beat the egg whites with a whisk or electric mixer until stiff. Gradually beat in the brown sugar. Spread this mixture evenly over the pastry. Top it all with the peanuts.

6. Bake for 30 to 35 minutes. Cool the pan on a wire rack. Cut into small squares when almost cool.

SARAH SAYS: When you beat the egg whites, add sugar, and then bake it, you are making a meringue. Look in other cookbooks under meringue, and you will see that there are all sorts of ways to use this light, sweet treat.

Totally Awesome Cookies!

Kids' All-Time Faves!

There are some cookies that come to mind instantly when you mention cookies — chocolate chip, oatmeal raisin, peanut butter — and that is just to name a few. In this chapter you will find recipes of old favorites and a few new "variations on old themes" that I added because they have become standbys for my friends and me. I hope you like these as much as we do!

Hugs & Kisses

The kisses are the chocolate candy kisses that go in the center of these great cookies, but can you guess what the hugs are? You're right if you said the cookie dough that you wrap around the kiss. Sprinkle with some confectioners' sugar and you have one very nice plate of cookies to serve up during movie night!

Prep time: 10 minutes to prepare the dough; refrigerate for at least 1 hour (up to 24 hours); final prep: 10 minutes

Pan: cookie sheets, greased

Oven: 375°F (190°C)

Makes: about 60 cookies

Ingredients:

2 sticks softened butter or margarine

$\frac{1}{2}$ cup (125 ml) granulated sugar

1 teaspoon (5 ml) vanilla extract

2 cups (500 ml) all-purpose flour

1 package (14 ounces/395 g) chocolate candy kisses

Confectioners' sugar (optional)

Putting it together:

Initial prep

1. Cream together the butter with the sugar until the dough is light and fluffy, using an electric mixer.

2. Add the vanilla and the flour. Blend well with a wooden spoon.

3. Cover the dough with a clean dish towel or waxed paper. Refrigerate the dough for at least 1 hour.

Final prep

1. Preheat the oven to 375°F (190°C).

2. Break off a walnut-sized piece of dough, roll it into a ball, and then flatten it with the palm of your hand, so it is not too thick.

3. Place a chocolate kiss in the center and fold the dough up around the kiss, pinching it shut so the kiss is covered completely.

4. Bake for 12 to 15 minutes until lightly browned. Cool the cookies on a wire rack.

Snickerdoodles

Other than Original Toll House Cookies — better known as chocolate
chip cookies — *Snickerdoodles* have got to be one of the all-time favorites. When
they are carefully baked just to the right degree of doneness, they are lightly browned
with a nice chewy interior. Right out of the oven, they are without equal!
No wonder kids of all ages love them!

Prep time: 20 minutes to prepare the dough;
refrigerate for at least 2 hours (up to 24 hours);
final prep: 15 minutes

Pan: cookie sheets, ungreased

Oven: 375°F (190°C)

Makes: about 60 cookies

Ingredients:

Pastry

$2\frac{3}{4}$ cups (675 ml) all-purpose flour

2 teaspoons (10 ml) cream of tartar
(it comes in a container like spices
are in)

1 teaspoon (5 ml) baking soda

$\frac{1}{2}$ teaspoon (2 ml) salt

1 cup (250 ml) solid vegetable shortening
(like Crisco)

$1\frac{1}{2}$ cups (375 ml) granulated sugar

2 eggs

Topping

2 tablespoons (30 ml) granulated sugar

2 teaspoons (10 ml) ground cinnamon

Putting it together:

Initial prep

1. In a large bowl, sift together the flour, cream of tartar, baking soda, and salt.

2. Cream together the shortening, sugar, and eggs until light and fluffy using
   an electric mixer.

3. Beat the flour mixture into the creamed ingredients until a dough-like batter forms.

4. Refrigerate the dough for at least 2 hours so it will be easy to handle.

Final prep

1. Preheat the oven to 375°F (190°C).

2. Stir the sugar and cinnamon together in a small bowl.

3. Roll pieces of the dough into walnut-sized balls, and then roll the balls in the cinnamon-sugar mixture. Place on a cookie sheet.

4. Bake 8 to 10 minutes, until lightly browned. Cool on a wire rack.

Taking a "study bake!"

Sarah's Quick Starts Tips!™

Chillin' Out

Some of these recipes require the dough to chill in the refrigerator for an hour or two — or as long as 24 hours. The amount of time isn't exact because the purpose is simply to let the dough chill enough so that it holds together when you work with it. What to do while waiting for the dough? You could quickly make the dough when you get home from school, refrigerate it while you do your chores or homework, and then after dinner, you can bake the cookies — we call it a "study bake" — when an adult is home to help. Or, follow the dough's example and just chill on out!

Best-Ever Peanut Butter & Chocolate Cookies

These cookies are guaranteed to make you the most popular person on the block. Luckily, this recipe yields plenty of cookies to share. Even better, if you have any left, these cookies remain "delish" for about a week when wrapped in foil.

Prep time: 15 minutes to prepare the dough; refrigerate for 1 hour (up to 24 hours); final prep: 15 minutes

Pan: cookie sheets, greased

Oven: 350°F (180°C)

Makes: about 95 cookies

Ingredients:

1 cup (250 ml) granulated sugar

1 cup (250 ml) packed light brown sugar

2 sticks softened butter or margarine

1 cup (250 ml) peanut butter, crunchy or smooth

2 eggs

2 cups (500 ml) all-purpose flour

1 teaspoon (5 ml) salt

1 teaspoon (5 ml) baking soda

1 teaspoon (5 ml) baking powder

1 teaspoon (5 ml) vanilla extract

1 package (10 ounce/285 g) M&M candies or 10 ounces (285 g) chocolate chunks

Putting it together:

Initial prep

1. Cream together the sugar, brown sugar, butter, peanut butter, and eggs in a large bowl.

2. Sift in the flour, salt, baking soda, and baking powder (called the dry ingredients).

3. Add the vanilla and M&M candies or chocolate chunks. Blend all the ingredients together.

4. Refrigerate the dough for an hour.

Final prep

1. Preheat the oven to 350°F (180°C).

2. Break the dough into walnut-sized pieces, and place on a cookie sheet.

3. Bake for 10 to 12 minutes. Cool on a wire rack.

Sarah's Quick Starts Tips!™

I scream,

You scream,

We all scream for ice cream … and cookies!

Can't decide if you're in the mood for ice cream or for cookies? Secretly in the mood for both? Then, treat yourself "real nice" by joining the two taste sensations together in an ice-cream cookie sandwich. Place a generous dollop of ice cream between two cookies and eat up! This one calls for plenty of napkins, so be prepared!

Chocolate Chip Crispers

I figure that most everyone can get the recipe for Original Toll House chocolate chip cookies right off the package of Nestle's chocolate chips. So instead, I've included a yummy chocolate chip cookie recipe that is sort of like eating a chocolate crunch bar.

Prep time: 30 minutes

Pan: cookie sheets, greased

Oven: 350°F (180°C)

Makes: about 52 cookies

Ingredients:

1 stick softened butter or margarine

1 cup (250 ml) granulated sugar

1 egg

1 teaspoon (5 ml) vanilla extract

$1\frac{1}{4}$ cups (300 ml) all-purpose flour

$\frac{1}{2}$ teaspoon (2 ml) baking soda

$\frac{1}{4}$ teaspoon (1 ml) salt

2 cups (500 ml) Rice Krispies or other puffed rice cereal

1 package (6 ounce/170 g) chocolate chips

Putting it together:

1. Preheat the oven to 350°F (180°C).

2. Cream together the butter and sugar in a large bowl until smooth, using an electric mixer.

3. Beat in the egg and vanilla.

4. In a separate bowl, combine the flour, baking soda, and salt. Mix well.

5. Add the flour mixture to the batter in the large bowl. Blend well.

6. Gently stir in the Rice Krispies and chocolate chips. Drop rounded tablespoonfuls onto the cookie sheets.

7. Bake for 12 minutes, or until light brown. Cool on a wire rack.

Sweet & Salty Cookies

Adults claim that the two best foods to combine are cheese and crackers. Kids on the other hand know better: The two yummiest treats in the world are chocolate and — no, not peanut butter — potato chips! What could be better than combining your favorite taste sensations into one fantastic cookie? Absolutely nothing!

Prep time: 15 minutes

Pan: cookie sheets, greased

Oven: 350°F (180°C)

Makes: about 50 cookies

Ingredients:

2 sticks softened butter or margarine

1 cup (250 ml) granulated sugar

1 cup (250 ml) packed light brown sugar

2 eggs

1 package (6 ounce/170 g) chocolate chips

1 bag (9 ounce/255 g) plain potato chips, crushed

$\frac{1}{2}$ cup (125 ml) nuts, coarsely chopped (optional)

2 cups (500 ml) all-purpose flour

1 teaspoon (5 ml) baking soda

Putting it together:

1. Preheat the oven to 350°F (180°C).

2. In a large bowl, cream together the butter, sugars, and eggs until light and fluffy, using an electric mixer. Then, stir in the chocolate chips, potato chips, nuts, and flour.

3. Shape the dough into walnut-sized pieces and place on a cookie sheet.

4. Bake for 10 to 12 minutes or until lightly browned. Cool on a wire rack.

SARAH SAYS: If the dough is too sticky to shape into pieces, chill it in the refrigerator for about $\frac{1}{2}$ hour before using.

Peanut Butter Cookies

Well, I think that *Peanut Butter Cookies* tie with *Snickerdoodles* (page 36) as the second most favorite cookie after chocolate chip. What do you think?

Prep time: 20 minutes to prepare the dough; refrigerate for at least 1 hour (up to 24 hours); final prep: 10 minutes

Pan: cookie sheets, greased

Oven: 350°F (180°C)

Makes: about 60 cookies

Ingredients:

1 cup (250 ml) packed light brown sugar

1 cup (250 ml) granulated sugar

2 sticks softened butter or margarine

1 cup (250 ml) peanut butter, crunchy or smooth

2 eggs

2 cups (500 ml) all-purpose flour

1 teaspoon (5 ml) salt

1 teaspoon (5 ml) baking soda

1 teaspoon (5 ml) baking powder

1 teaspoon (5 ml) vanilla extract

Yummy options:

Add one of these or some of each:

1 cup (250 ml) salted peanuts, coarsely chopped

1 cup (250 ml) chocolate chunks

Putting it together:

Initial prep

1. In a large bowl, cream together the brown and granulated sugars, the butter, peanut butter, and eggs until well blended, using an electric mixer.

2. In another bowl, sift together the flour, salt, baking soda, and baking powder and gradually add it to the butter mixture.

Bake the Best-Ever Cookies!

3. Add the vanilla, and blend thoroughly. Stir in the options you selected.

4. Chill the dough for at least 1 hour.

Final prep

1. Preheat the oven to 350° (180°C). Break the dough into walnut-sized pieces and place on the cookie sheet. Press each cookie with the back of a greased fork, to make a grid-like pattern (a peanut butter cookie tradition).

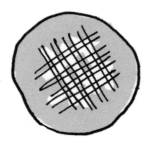 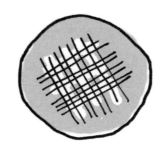 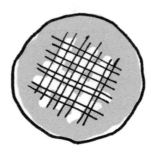

2. Bake for 10 to 12 minutes. Cool on wire racks.

Sarah's Quick Starts Tips!™

Making Colossal Cookies

OK, as we all know, bigger does not always mean better. However, when it comes to cookies, the matter is up for debate. Sure, regular cookies are great, but colossal cookies are positively awesome!

For most drop cookie recipes, prepare the cookie dough as usual, except drop the dough onto the cookie sheet from a $\frac{1}{4}$-cup (50 ml) measuring cup, placing them about 4" (10 cm) apart and at least 2" (5 cm) from the sides. Add about an extra minute onto the baking time, or bake until the edges are lightly browned. These are general instructions, so you might have to experiment a little bit. Depending on the recipe, it can make anywhere from 12 to 20 colossal-sized cookies.

Making It Special with Cookies!

Everyone thinks of cookies for Christmas and maybe for Valentine's Day, too, but why stop there? Don't you think it would be fun to bake some *Save-the-Earth Drop Cookies* for Earth Day or Green-Up Day, some fresh blueberry cookies for Fourth of July, and a bouquet of *Bloomin' Flowers* for Mother's Day? Well, turn the page, because although cookies can make any day special, here are some fantastic cookies for those very special days — especially for you!

Bake the Best-Ever Cookies!

Nice Mice

When Halloween rolls around and the field mice begin making their presence known in our garage, we make these "spicy micey" cookies! They smell so good and they taste just right for a Happy Halloween treat!

Prep time: 20 minutes to prepare the dough; refrigerate for at least 1 hour; final prep: 30 minutes

Pan: cookie sheets, greased

Oven: 350°F (180°C)

Makes: about 20 mice

Ingredients:

Favorite Cut-Out Sugar Cookies dough (see pages 56–57)

$\frac{1}{4}$ teaspoon (1 ml) ground cinnamon

$\frac{1}{4}$ teaspoon (1 ml) ground allspice

Decorative topping:

1 egg, beaten with a spoonful of water

Raisins

Sliced almonds

Chow mein noodles

Putting it together:

Initial prep

Prepare the sugar cookie dough according to the directions on pages 56–57, adding the cinnamon and allspice to the dry ingredients in the recipe.

Final prep

1. Preheat the oven to 350°F (180°C).

2. Roll large walnut-sized pieces of dough into small egg shapes. Place the ovals about 2" (5 cm) apart on the cookie sheets. Moisten the top of the dough with the beaten egg and water. Cut the raisins in half, rolling each piece into a ball for the eyes. Add the sliced almonds for the ears. Insert the chow mein noodle for the tail.

3. Bake for 15 to 20 minutes, until lightly browned. Let stand briefly and then move to a wire rack to complete cooling. To serve, put on an orange plate or napkin.

SARAH SAYS: Spices are expensive to buy. If you don't have ground allspice, maybe you can borrow a little from a neighbor, or simply do without it.

Save-the-Earth Drop Cookies

(Filled with homemade gorp. Munch on these on Green-Up Day!)

OK, so these cookies may not actually save the earth, but they are wholesome and will give you and your friends an energy boost, as you join your community in cleaning up on Green-Up Day!

Prep time: 20 minutes

Pan: cookie sheets, greased

Oven: 350°F (180°C)

Makes: about 24 cookies

Ingredients:

$1\frac{1}{2}$ sticks melted butter or margarine

1 cup (250 ml) granulated sugar

$\frac{1}{4}$ cup (50 ml) molasses

1 lightly beaten egg

$1\frac{3}{4}$ cups (425 ml) all-purpose flour

$\frac{1}{2}$ teaspoon (2 ml) ground cloves

$\frac{1}{2}$ teaspoon (2 ml) ground ginger

1 teaspoon (5 ml) ground cinnamon

$\frac{1}{2}$ teaspoon (2 ml) salt

$\frac{1}{2}$ teaspoon (2 ml) baking soda

$1\frac{1}{2}$ cups (375 ml) homemade gorp (see next page)

Putting it together:

1. Preheat the oven to 350°F (180°C).

2. In a large bowl, combine the melted butter, sugar, and molasses. Then, add the lightly beaten egg.

3. Set aside the gorp. In a separate bowl, sift together all of the other remaining ingredients. Add gradually to your molasses mixture and mix thoroughly. Lastly, stir in the gorp.

4. Place rounded spoonfuls of dough on the cookie sheets. Bake 8 to 10 minutes until cookies begin to brown, but take them out while still soft (you don't want them to be too crunchy). Cool on a wire rack.

SARAH SAYS: This is a great recipe to be sure to put ingredients away as you use them. That way, when the instructions tell you to add all of the remaining ingredients, you will know exactly which ones you haven't used yet.

Bake the Best-Ever Cookies!

Great Gorp!

This snack is a favorite among hikers and other athletes who strive to go the distance. Why not pack this good source of energy into some incredible cookies? Use it in *Save-the-Earth Drop Cookies* and try it as a mix-in with other recipes, too!

Ingredients:

2 cups (500 ml) unsalted roasted peanuts

1 cup (250 ml) raisins

$\frac{1}{2}$ cup (125 ml) shredded coconut

1 cup (250 ml) dried cranberries

1 cup (250 ml) chocolate chips

1 cup (250 ml) dried banana chips or assorted dried fruit mix

Putting it together:

1. Combine all of the ingredients in a large bag and shake gently.

2. Store in a tightly sealed jar or zip-locking plastic bag.

Making It Special!

Bloomin' Flowers

(lemon-flavored flowers on a stick)

This is such a great cookie to make for all sorts of fun: Make flowers on stick stems, Christmas trees on stick trunks, Halloween ghosts on sticks, shamrocks on sticks — the recipe stays the same! You just cut out your own cardboard template and color and flavor the dough as you choose. A lot of fun for the baker and the recipient!

Prep time: 20 minutes to prepare the dough; refrigerate for 1 to 2 hours (up to 24 hours); final prep: 20 minutes

Pan: cookie sheets, ungreased

Oven: 375°F (190°C)

Makes: about 12 cookies

Ingredients:

$\frac{2}{3}$ cup (150 ml) solid vegetable shortening (like Crisco)

6 tablespoons (90 ml) softened butter or margarine

$\frac{3}{4}$ cup (175 ml) granulated sugar

$\frac{3}{4}$ cup (175 ml) packed light brown sugar

2 eggs

2 teaspoons (10 ml) vanilla extract

1 teaspoon (5 ml) lemon juice concentrate, ground cinnamon, or other flavoring of your choice

$3\frac{1}{2}$ cups (875 ml) all-purpose flour

2 teaspoons (10 ml) baking powder

1 teaspoon (5 ml) salt

Putting it together:

Initial prep

1. In a large bowl, cream together the shortening, butter, granulated sugar, and brown sugar, using an electric mixer. Then, beat in the eggs, vanilla, and lemon juice.

2. In another bowl, stir together the flour, baking powder, and salt; gradually add this to the butter mixture, blending thoroughly. Cover the dough tightly with plastic wrap and refrigerate for 1 to 2 hours.

3. Meanwhile, cut the cookie patterns from lightweight cardboard, choosing simple shapes and making them 5" to 6" (12.5 to 15 cm) wide at most. Also have ready Popsicle sticks or craft sticks.

Final prep

1. Preheat the oven to 375°F (190°C).

2. Roll out the dough, a little at a time, on a floured surface to a thickness of about $\frac{1}{4}$" (5 mm). Refrigerate the extra dough, until you are ready to use it.

3. Place the patterns on the dough and cut around the edges with a dull knife. Remove the patterns; using a wide metal spatula, transfer the cookies carefully to the cookie sheets, spacing them 2" (5 cm) apart. Insert a Popsicle stick about 2" (5 cm) into the base of each cookie.

4. Bake for 12 to 15 minutes, or until very lightly browned. Cool the cookies on wire racks.

5. While the cookies cool, prepare the decorator's icing in colors if you wish (see page 58). Decorate the cookies with icing or toppings of your choice.

SARAH SAYS: Be very cautious when moving your cookies to and from the cookie sheet. To store these to give as gifts, let the icing dry completely. Then wrap in colorful cellophane and tie with a ribbon. For a Mother's Day, Father's Day, or May Day surprise, tuck a few wild flowers into a ribbon tied around the Popsicle stick.

Make a Cookie Bouquet!

Before rolling out the dough for the flowers, add a scant drop of food coloring to the dough for each flower, making a bouquet of different colored flowers. To make a pattern for *Bloomin' Flowers*, simply trace around a circle about 2" (5 cm) for the center of the flower. Add smaller half circles about $\frac{1}{2}$"(1 cm) wide (about the size of a soda bottle cap) for the petals. "Paste" the petals all around the large circle by pressing the edges together, using a dab of water on your fingers. Insert the Popsicle stick stem and bake as directed. Let cool slightly on the pan before moving to a wire rack to cool.

Twist & Shape Cookies

(A great cookie to twist and shape into year-round shapes, colors, and flavors.)

Make these into peppermint *Candy Cane Cookies*, cinnamon *Star of David Cookies*, or *Dad's Day Cookies* (flavored and colored to please your dad). To turn these delicious and festive cookies into a very special gift, wrap two or three cookies in some clear cellophane and tie with a colorful ribbon to match the color you've woven into the cookies. A perfectly perfect gift from you!

Prep time: 35 minutes

Pan: cookie sheets, ungreased

Oven: 375F° (190°C)

Makes: about 48 cookies, depending on your design

Ingredients:

1 stick softened butter or margarine

$\frac{1}{2}$ cup (125 ml) solid vegetable shortening (like Crisco)

1 cup (250 ml) confectioners' sugar

1 egg

1 teaspoon (5 ml) vanilla extract

$1\frac{1}{2}$ teaspoons (7 ml) dough flavoring (see page 53)

$2\frac{1}{2}$ cups (625 ml) all-purpose flour

1 teaspoon (5 ml) salt

$\frac{1}{2}$ teaspoon (2 ml) food coloring (to match your design)

$\frac{1}{2}$ cup (125 ml) topping flavoring (see page 53)

$\frac{1}{2}$ cup (125 ml) granulated sugar

Putting it together:

1. Preheat the oven to 375°F (190°C).

2. Mix the butter, shortening, confectioners' sugar, egg, vanilla, and dough flavoring together thoroughly.

3. Blend in the flour and salt.

4. If the dough is sticky, refrigerate for an hour or so. Divide the dough in half; blend the food coloring into one half of the dough.

... continued on next page

5. Shape 1 to 2 teaspoons (5 to 10 ml) of dough at a time into 4"- (10 cm) long ropes. For smooth, even ropes, roll them back and forth on a lightly floured surface.

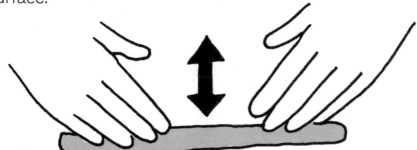

6. To twist, place one of each color rope side by side; press them together lightly and twist.

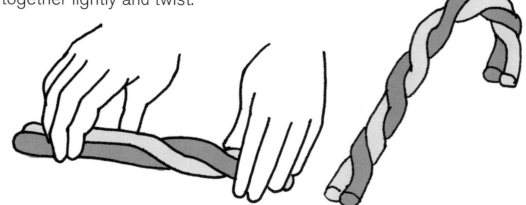

Then, select a shape to make (candy cane, Star of David, letters for DAD, butterfly wings, etc.). Complete one cookie at a time.

7 Mix your topping flavoring or candy and the granulated sugar together. Set aside. Bake the cookies 10 minutes, or until very lightly browned.

8. Immediately sprinkle cookies with candy mixture (while still on cookie sheets). Cool on wire racks.

SARAH SAYS: Some flavorings are stronger than others are. When you add flavorings, start with the amount suggested in the general recipe and then adjust in the future, if necessary. When you bake your shapes, remember that the more open your design is, the faster it will bake. Check at about 8 minutes, until you know for sure.

Twist & Shape Ideas

Experiment with this cookie to see if you can come up with 12 months of flavors, colors, and shapes.

Here are a few I have used:

Candy Cane Shapes:

Food coloring: **red**

Dough flavoring: **almond extract**

Topping flavoring: **crushed peppermint candies**

Dad's Day Shapes:

Spell the word Dad, using three twisted ropes. Use Dad's favorite color, flavor, and toppings.

Star of David Shapes:

Food coloring: **blue**

Dough flavoring: **lemon concentrate**

Topping flavoring: **cinnamon and sugar**

Heart Shapes:

Food coloring: **red**

Dough flavoring: **grated orange rind**

Topping flavoring: **crushed red hot hearts**

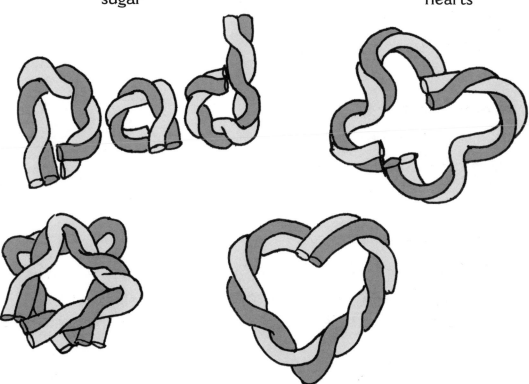

Making It Special!

Fourth-of-July Cookies

(a summery lemon cookie with blueberries)

Fourth of July has always been a big holiday in my family, complete with swimming, a picnic to end all picnics, fireworks, the *1812 Overture*, John Philip Sousa, lots of marching around with flags — and best of all, good times shared with aunts, uncles, cousins, and friends. And what would a weekend of fun be like without a special cookie? Well, I'm sure I can't imagine!

Prep time: 20 minutes

Pan: cookie sheets, greased

Oven: 375°F (190°C)

Makes: about 36 cookies

Ingredients:

1 stick softened butter or margarine

1 egg

1 cup (250 ml) granulated sugar

$1\frac{1}{2}$ (7 ml) teaspoons grated lemon peel

2 cups (500 ml) all-purpose flour

2 teaspoons (10 ml) baking powder

$\frac{1}{2}$ teaspoon (2 ml) salt

$\frac{1}{4}$ cup (50 ml) milk

1 cup (250 ml) fresh or canned blueberries, washed and drained

Confectioners' sugar

For Red, White, and Blue Cookies:

Add $\frac{1}{2}$ teaspoon (2 ml) red food coloring in step 3.

Fresh blueberries: Press a plump fresh blueberry on top after sprinkling with confectioners' sugar in step 5.

Putting it together:

1. Preheat the oven to 375°F (190°C).

2. In a large bowl, cream the butter with the egg, using an electric mixer. Gradually add the sugar and then the lemon peel, beating until it's blended.

Bake the Best-Ever Cookies!

3. In another bowl, stir together the flour, baking powder, and salt; add this to the butter mixture, alternating with the milk (a little flour, a little milk), blending it thoroughly. Add the food coloring now, if you wish. Gently fold in the blueberries, being careful not to crush them.

4. Drop rounded spoonfuls of the dough onto the cookie sheet.

5. Bake for 15 minutes, or until golden brown. Cool on wire racks. After 5 minutes, sift the confectioners' sugar lightly over the cookies. Top with blueberries now, if you wish. Serve warm or let them cool completely.

SARAH SAYS: These cookies are at their prime while still warm, so you might want to plan to eat them soon after baking. You can prepare the dough in advance and refrigerate it; then, bake the cookies at the last minute. Use fresh blueberries if you can.

Favorite Cut-Out Sugar Cookies

For a year of creative cooking fun, this recipe makes wonderful cut-out sugar cookies! Top them with plain granulated sugar, colored sugar crystals, cookie icing — or other fanciful, fun toppings. Think big in terms of cut-outs: moon and stars, circus animals, flower shapes, snowflakes, and butterflies. And that's just for starters!

See page 45 to make spicy *Nice Mice* cookies using this sugar cookie recipe.

Prep time: 20 minutes to prepare the dough; refrigerate for at least 1 hour (up to 24 hours); final prep: varies

Pan: cookie sheets, ungreased

Oven: 375°F (190°C)

Makes: about 48 cookies

Ingredients:

$1\frac{1}{2}$ sticks softened butter or margarine

1 cup (250 ml) granulated sugar

2 eggs

1 teaspoon (5 ml) vanilla extract

$2\frac{3}{4}$ cups (675 ml) all-purpose flour

1 teaspoon (5 ml) baking powder

1 teaspoon (5 ml) salt

Topping of your choice

Yummy toppings:

Granulated sugar

Colored sugar crystals

Rainbow-colored sprinkles

Decorator's icing (see page 58)

Cinnamon-sugar mixture

Putting it together:

Initial prep

1. In a large bowl, cream the butter and sugar together, using an electric mixer. Next, beat in the eggs and vanilla.

2. In another bowl, stir the flour, baking powder, and salt together. Gradually add the flour mixture to the butter mixture, blending into a soft dough. Refrigerate the dough for at least an hour.

Final prep

1. Preheat the oven to 375°F (190°C).

2. To roll out for cookie-cutter use: Roll out some of the dough (keep the rest refrigerated) on a lightly floured surface to a thickness of about $\frac{1}{8}$" (2 mm).

3. Cut out shapes and carefully move them to an ungreased cookie sheet (I use a metal spatula so I don't break the shape). Bake for 7 to 10 minutes until very lightly browned. Sprinkle on toppings other than chocolate or icing (wait until cool for those). Cool on wire racks.

SARAH SAYS: No cookie cutters handy? Make your own by using a glass, a jar lid, even a milk bottle cap or a soda bottle cap. Mix and match. Or, make a template out of cereal-box cardboard and cut around it with a dull knife for a cookie-cutter shape of your own design!

The Keys to Cookie-Cutter Success!

If working with cookie cutters has always caused you problems, you have lots of company. Here are the keys to making really nice cookies:

* Keep your dough chilled as you work and re-chill extra dough that you gather after making shapes, before rolling it out again.

* Cut on a lightly floured surface so the dough won't stick.

* Roll out the dough to $\frac{1}{8}$" (2 mm) thickness. If the dough is too thick the cookies will need to bake longer, turning too brown, plus they don't look quite as nice.

* Use cookie cutters with sharp edges.

(See *Lemon-Poppy Seed Way-Cool Treats*, page 29, for another cookie-cutter recipe.)

Decorator's Icing

This is simple to make and much, much better than store-bought. Add $\frac{1}{4}$ teaspoon (1 ml) vanilla extract to 1 cup (250 ml) sifted confectioners' sugar. Stir in some milk or orange juice — only 1 teaspoon (5 ml) at a time — until the icing is of a drizzling consistency. Makes $\frac{1}{2}$ cup (125 ml).

To make these cookies even more fun, divide the icing into separate bowls and add a drop or two of food coloring.

To use the icing from a tube, make it thicker by adding less liquid or by beginning with 2 cups (500 ml) sifted confectioners' sugar. To make your own tube for "drawing" on your cookies, fill a small zip-locking plastic bag with some frosting. Close it tightly. Snip off one lower corner of the bag with a pair of scissors — only a very, very tiny snip — and squeeze it as you draw!

An original piece of edible art by you!

Sparkling Sun Catchers

To hang your sun catchers so they can catch some multicolored rays, use a toothpick to put a small hole in the top of the cookie before you bake it. Then, once the cookies cool completely, thread with strong thread to hang in the window.

Prep time: 10 minutes to prepare the dough;
refrigerate for 1 to 2 hours;
final prep: 25 minutes

Pan: cookie sheets, lined with aluminum foil

Oven: 375°F (190°C)

Makes: 36 to 48 cookies

Ingredients:

3 tablespoons (45 ml) softened butter
or margarine

$\frac{1}{3}$ cup (75 ml) solid vegetable shortening
(like Crisco)

2 cups (500 ml) all-purpose flour

1 egg

$\frac{3}{4}$ cup (175 ml) granulated sugar

1 tablespoon (15 ml) milk

1 teaspoon (5 ml) baking powder

1 teaspoon (5 ml) vanilla extract

Dash salt

$\frac{1}{2}$ cup (125 ml) finely crushed
hard candy

Putting it together:

Initial prep

1. In a large bowl, beat the butter and shortening together with an electric mixer on medium to high speed for 30 seconds.

2. Add about half of the flour, the egg, sugar, milk, baking powder, vanilla, and salt. Beat until thoroughly combined.

3. Beat in the remaining flour. Cover the dough with a clean dish towel or waxed paper. Refrigerate the dough for 1 to 2 hours.

... continued on next page

Final prep

1. Preheat the oven to 375°F (190°C).

2. On a lightly floured surface, roll out half of the dough at a time to a thickness of about $\frac{1}{8}$" (2.5 mm). Cut into desired shapes with a $2\frac{1}{2}$" (6 cm) cookie cutter or a template of your own design. Place the cookies on a foil-lined cookie sheet. Cut out small shapes in the centers of the cookies, removing the dough. Spoon some candy into each center to fill the holes.

3. Bake for 7 to 8 minutes, or until the cookie edges are firm and the bottoms are very lightly browned. Cool on wire racks.

SARAH SAYS: These are lots of fun to bake no matter what your age. Little kids that you baby-sit will especially like making them, but whole families like to get in the act, too. For added fun, outline your cookies or the shapes in the center with Decorator's Icing (see recipe, page 58).

Sarah's Quick Starts Tips!™

Catch the Sun!

These are fun all-year round. They make great Easter cookies or spring-time cookies. In fact, to celebrate birthdays or other special days, cut out the shapes you like and add candy to match the celebration you are planning. Invite guests or family members to each choose one to hang in their own rooms to bring some sparkle into their days!

Index

Bake the Best-Ever Cookies!